BRITAIN IN OLD PHOTOGRAPHS

LUTON

STUART SMITH

ALAN SUTTON PUBLISHING LIMITED

Alan Sutton Publishing Limited
Phoenix Mill · Far Thrupp · Stroud
Gloucestershire · GL5 2BU

First published 1995

Cover photographs: (front) The Central Café,
Cheapside, *c.* 1920; (back) reconstructing a
traffic accident at the corner of George Street
and Cheapside, 1924.
Title page photograph: George Street from the
old Town Hall, *c.* 1900.

British Library Cataloguing in Publication Data.
A catalogue record for this book is available from
the British Library.

ISBN 0-7509-0936-6

Typeset in 9/10 Sabon.
Typesetting and origination by
Alan Sutton Publishing Limited.
Printed in Great Britain by
WBC Ltd, Bridgend.

The Carnegie Library and the Midland Hotel, 1956. This area is now part of St
George's Square.

Contents

The engineering drawing office, Vauxhall Motors, 1931.

Introduction

The town of Luton lies among the Chiltern Hills in a valley formed partly by the action of glaciers during the Ice Age. The first occupants settled in the area at around the time that the ice sheets were receding to the north. This is proved by the thousands of Palaeolithic flint tools that have been found there during the last hundred years, the great majority being unearthed by the notable Worthington G. Smith during the last decades of the nineteenth century. The Romans and Saxons, too, were known to have settled at Luton, especially to the north of the present town in the areas now covered by Leagrave and Biscot.

Some of the first written accounts of the town date from the early tenth century, when it was described as consisting of a few houses surrounding a church at Park Square. The Domesday Book of 1087 lists Luton as having a population of about 700, a weekly market, and no fewer than seven windmills. The town's economy was based on farming and agriculture; the market that formed an integral part of the medieval town provided not only revenue collected by tolls, but also gave an outlet for the crafts and goods that the community produced. By the late seventeenth century, two other important trades were being followed to complement the work carried out on the land. Brewing took place on many of the large estates and farms and was gradually becoming centralized as a result of the actions of astute brewers; these would later be responsible for laying the foundations of a brewing empire based in the town. The plaiting of straw and the making of straw hats was an industry for which Luton became famous, and it was to provide employment and ultimately housing for thousands of people, both local and from the neighbouring hamlets.

By the early nineteenth century, much of the plaiting was carried out as a cottage industry in the rural areas, while the sewing, which was better paid, was concentrated in the town. It was from this time that present-day Luton began to develop. As late as 1801, its main street, George Street, was a narrow hedge-lined lane housing several ancient inns and farms. When the prospering hat manufacturers required space for their factories and warehouses they chose George Street; land was readily and cheaply available there, and it was easily accessible to their employees, most of whom were female. Many of their buildings still stand, forming the basic structure of the modern shops and stores.

From the 1830s numerous businesses grew as a result of the straw hat trade. Apart from directly associated firms such as bleachers, dyers, and sewing machine manufacturers, many others sprang up: various builders, timber merchants, bricklayers, and land speculators were all involved in building the new houses required by the influx of workers. New districts to the east and west of the centre, High Town and New Town, were both started, but unfortunately, because of lack of adequate planning and poor materials, within twenty years some of this housing was already considered unfit for human habitation. It was to be another one hundred years before some of these properties were vacated in the town's early redevelopment projects.

Until the 1870s the churches had provided schooling, but on the election of the School Board and the following compulsory education, many new schools were built and places made available. Unfortunately, very few of these original schools escaped the ravages of time and the bulldozers of the 1970s.

Coinciding with a downturn in the straw hat trade, the Luton Chamber of Commerce was founded in 1877 to try to solve the problem of male unemployment. A concerted publicity campaign promised cheap electricity, low rates, and an abundance of inexpensive land, and the recently opened Great Northern Railway link was nearby. As a result many new industries, which were to change the economic, industrial, and social fabric of the town, relocated to Luton. Some of the early arrivals included Haywood Tyler (pump manufacturers), Laporte's, CWS Cocoa Works, The British Gelatine Works, Commercial Cars (later Commer), Davies Gas Stove Company, George Kent's, SKF Bearing Company, and in 1905 Vauxhall Motors, which was to become the largest employer in the area.

During the 1920s and 1930s many of Luton's older industries and trades began to decline, but the newer industries expanded, helping to build a thriving engineering town. This helped to attract other firms such as Electrolux and Percival Aircraft, the latter of which set up on a grass runway that was to become the site of the huge London Luton Airport, now one of the region's largest employers.

Great changes in the face of the town began in the 1950s with the first phase of the redevelopment of sub-standard dwellings in High Town, followed in the next ten years by similar work in New Town and in the vicinity of the parish church. After several tenders had been submitted during the early 1960s, the Council awarded the Arndale Development Company the contract to build a 'state of the art' indoor shopping centre. Building began before the decade was out. In the minds of many Lutonians, this destroyed the heart of the town: many notable buildings were lost, including the public baths and swimming pool, the Grand Theatre, several schools, many old and ancient inns, and the by now run down heart of the hat trade. The new Arndale was proclaimed as being the largest in-town covered shopping complex in Europe, and indeed provided new outlets for many differing retailers, all trading in a characterless and clinical environment.

The town continues to expand and now encompasses the hamlets which forty years ago considered themselves quite separate. The local government rehousing projects, coupled with private development, have pushed the populated districts right up to the town boundaries, losing much good agricultural land, to provide space for a population that has risen from 36,000 in 1901 to a peak of 171,000 in 1991.

Apart from the towns and cities that suffered badly from enemy bombing during the Second World War, Luton has probably lost more Victorian streets and important buildings as a result of redevelopment than any other area in Great Britain. The following pages contain many pictures of Luton from the period before the planner and bulldozer took over. Many of the photographs are published for the first time; they conjure up a nostalgic journey for Lutonians and provide an insight to the town for students of town planning and urban development.

Section One

TOWN VIEWS

Chambers's shop, Market Hill, 1867.

The Grand Theatre, Waller Street, *c*. 1955. Built in 1898, it was opened by the actress Lily Langtry in December of that year, and its first production was Wilson Barratt's *The Sign of the Cross*. The interior decor was typical of late Victorian theatres, featuring stage-side boxes, seating for one thousand people in the stalls, circle, and upper circle, and much decorative plaster-work. During the first forty years of its active life, the regular performances were well supported by Lutonians and drew audiences from as far afield as London. Until recently, the wall of the Red Lion Hotel in Castle Street bore a steel sign inscribed 'To the Grand Theatre' to direct theatre-goers from London and the south. The Grand began to lose some of its attraction after the end of the Second World War and saw out its last days with productions of pantomime and semi-nude reviews. It was demolished in 1962, to be replaced by a Tesco supermarket, which was itself demolished in 1973 during the second phase of the Arndale development.

Market Day in Park Square, *c.* 1910. Luton had held a regular market day since at least the time when the Saxons had settled in the area. By the late nineteenth century the market occupied Park Square and Market Hill. The plait market, which had traded in George Street, had already gone under cover in the Plait Halls.

Park Square, *c.* 1910. The market remained on this site until 1925, when it moved indoors to the redundant Plait Halls. This photograph is taken looking south down Park Street and features, on the left, the Luton Modern School, built in 1908 as the Edward the Seventh School on the site of the Burr family brewery (see page 94). The school was demolished in 1957 and replaced by Luton Technical College, now the University of Luton.

Park Street from Park Square, *c.* 1925. All the buildings on the left have since disappeared, and the low-roofed building at centre right is the Cock Inn, a seventeenth-century coaching inn, which first found mention around the time of the great plague of 1665. The building at the extreme right has now been incorporated into the Brewery Tap public house and is, along with the Cock Inn, one of the town's most popular evening meeting places.

A general view of Park Square, *c.* 1906. The photograph was taken before the arrival of the electric tram service. None of the buildings shown are still standing, although those on the left, dating from 1760, were re-faced to similar designs in the 1980s. The shops, centre rear, were demolished in 1976.

Park Square, 1957. This row of shops, which included the Technical School, was earmarked for demolition so as to allow the building and development of a brand new Technical College. While the school and shops continued to operate, the College was built to their rear. From this front view there is no trace of what is happening behind them.

Within weeks of the previous photograph, the buildings were demolished so that the college could be completed. The partly finished building almost hides the parish church of St Mary, which had until then been one of the most prominent structures in the town. Johnson's café moved to Castle Street, where it traded for another decade before the proprietor retired.

Park Street West, 1950s. The street was originally laid out in around 1875 to provide building land for some very substantial private dwellings, and it also gave access to the Phoenix Brewery, which had been brewing for John William Green since 1869. Previously access to the brewery had been via a narrow thoroughfare known as Middle Row and situated at Market Hill. The brewery was demolished in 1977, with the site now occupied by the modern offices of Whitbread Inns.

Market Hill, 1956. Only one building remains standing today, and that is the public house at the extreme right. It has recently been renamed The Rat and Carrot, but was formerly known as The Crown, The Nickel Bag and Heights. The tall building formed part of Blundell's home furnishing business. The Market Hill entrance to the covered market was through a narrow passage alongside the extended shop awning.

Market Hill, 1970. The Conservative Club was built in 1908 to replace an earlier and smaller club on the same site. With the increase in the number of motor cars, parking for club members became a problem, partly because cars from a nearby taxi rank tended to spill over on to club property. This prime town centre site was sold in 1975 to help finance the building of a new club near Old Bedford Road. The old club was demolished that same year.

Market Hill, 1867. The proprietors of Chambers's shop may here have been posing for the photographer for the last time, for this complete site was cleared later that year. The triangular site consisted of the original Corn Market House, built early in the eighteenth century, an ancient inn and brewhouse, and various shops and small dwellings.

Market Hill, 1910. This photograph was taken from the same position as the previous one and shows the splendid mock-Gothic Corn Exchange that replaced the ramshackle buildings demolished forty-three years earlier. It was originally used as a corn chandlery, but also saw service as the Court-Leet and as a place for public meetings, exhibitions and concerts. During the building's later years, the ground floor was taken over by the White Rose Café. It was found to have structural defects and so was deemed unsafe for the public, resulting in its being pulled down in 1951.

George Street and Chapel Street corner, *c.* 1896. Chapel Street was formerly known as Hog Lane. In 1897 the entire right-hand side of the street was demolished for road widening, with the loss of the Star Tea Company building, which had once been the premises of a straw hat merchant. On that corner was built the London and County Bank, later the National Westminster Bank. The building on the left was rebuilt as Boot's the Chemist, a very popular shop with Lutonians.

Market Hill from George Street, by now the main street of the town, *c.* 1900. Boot's the Chemist was still to acquire the upper storey, and the London and County Bank building was only one year old. There were still hat factories in George Street at the turn of the century, even though the industry was in decline.

Market Hill, 1977. This fine red-brick building was built on the site of John Waller's gardens, known locally as the 'Pleasure Gardens'. John Waller was one of five sons, three of whom were influential in the development of the town. All the family were involved in the straw plait and hat industry, and owned substantial property within the town. John's nine acres of land were sold by his executors after his death, and his 'pleasure gardens' soon became the heart of industrial Luton.

Cheapside, *c.* 1906. This photograph of Luton's first head post office was taken by T.G. Hobbs, who was responsible for recording many of the early images of the town. The post office was built in 1881 on land that had belonged to John Waller. By the time these postmen were photographed as they paraded for morning roll call and letter collection, the office was no longer able to handle adequately the amount of business provided by the growing town. Even so, it was to be another seventeen years before a new head post office was built, by which time the Cheapside building was finding it impossible to cope. After the business was transferred to Upper George Street, the premises were used by the Herts and Beds Bacon Factory as a retail butcher's shop. For some time the upper floors saw use as a private club, but during the last few years of its existence the building stood empty and neglected, before falling victim to the bulldozer in 1973. In its prime, it was one of the finest properties in Cheapside.

Cheapside, 1910. Together with Bute Street and Waller Street, Cheapside formed the very heart of Luton's hat industry, with many small associated businesses located here. These companies included sewing machine manufacturers, cotton and ribbon makers, and block makers. The Plait Halls, where the buying and selling of the raw materials took place, were also here.

A similar view taken in 1960 showing plainly that little has changed. The post office is now the Herts and Beds Bacon Factory, and the clothing shop on the right has become part of Blundell Brothers. The former hat factories at the far end of the street are the only buildings visible that remain today.

Cheapside, 1930. The covered market, five years after moving into the old Plait Halls following the decline of the straw hat industry. These were built in 1868, the foundation stone being laid by Mr A.P. Welsh, a local plait dealer and philanthropist. In 1897 Queen Victoria's Diamond Jubilee was celebrated by the giving of a dinner in the halls for the aged and poor of the town. Along with the rest of this top end of Cheapside the buildings were demolished in 1973.

Chapel Street, 1926. Called Hog Lane until the middle of the nineteenth century, it had been a narrow lane with many sub-standard dwellings. It was widened in 1897, when the left side of the street was pulled down and replaced by the buildings shown. The Queen's Head public house was rebuilt on the same site. Apart from the trams, the view remains very much unchanged to this day.

George Street, July 1900. This was Luton's main street and shopping centre until the opening of the Arndale in the mid-1970s. Less than one hundred years before this photograph was taken, George Street had been a narrow hedge-lined lane with several ancient inns and farms. The first new buildings were erected by the hat manufacturers in around 1830, but it was to be eighty more years before retail shops were to appear.

George Street, c. 1926. Little has changed from the previous photograph except that the Town Hall at the far end has gone.

George Street, 1910. The Town Hall was built in 1847 by the Town Hall Company. It was sold to the Board of Health, the forerunner to the Council, in 1876, and became more like a modern Town Hall, with rooms for various Council departments. At this time the offices occupied only the central building, a public house standing on one side and a retail shop on the other. By the turn of the century the whole site had been acquired and incorporated into the Town Hall.

George Street, 20 July 1919. The Town Hall suffered at the hands of a mob, which included some disenchanted ex-servicemen, at the end of the Peace Day celebrations held the previous day. It was felt by many that they had been treated badly when the Celebration Committee excluded them from some of the events they had arranged. There had also been much bad feeling building up towards the Council over the years. This animosity got out of hand on the night of 19 July, resulting in a riot and the burning down of the Town Hall. Luton remained without a central Council meeting place until the present Town Hall was opened in 1936.

George Street, *c.* 1910, featuring the George Hotel, an early sixteenth-century coaching inn. It was undoubtedly one of the town's oldest inns, and between the wars was a popular venue for dinner-dances. Regular weekday and weekend functions were held in the hotel right up to 1965, when it was closed and demolished. The site is now occupied by a Littlewoods store.

The new Town Hall was six years in the future when this photograph was taken in 1930. The war memorial was unveiled by Lady Ludlow on 10 December 1922, its cost of £4,000 having been raised by public subscription.

The Carnegie Library on the corner of George Street and Williamson Street, 1956. Built in 1910 as a generous gift from the American steel magnate Andrew Carnegie, it replaced the Free Library, which had become totally inadequate in serving the growing town. It was designed by a local architect, B.C. Deacon, and was opened by Carnegie in October 1910, serving the town well until 1962, when it was replaced by the present Central Library. Its demolition that same year was a great architectural loss to the town.

The Carnegie Library and the Midland Hotel, 1956. The hotel was built for John Pugh of Windsor in 1868 on the corner of Manchester Street and Williamson Street. It was run successfully until around 1928, when part of the building was leased to an insurance company as offices and another part to a ladies' gown shop business. The hotel then occupied only a small portion of the building, with an entrance in Williamson Street. The site was cleared in 1976 together with the entire eastern side of Manchester Street, and it now forms part of St George's Square.

George Street, from the tower of the Town Hall, *c.* 1960. The street later became traffic-free as a result of a project early in the 1990s. At the bottom right is Wellington Street, and the chimney and tall buildings on the skyline formed part of J.W. Green's Phoenix Brewery, although by 1960 it was brewing under the banner of Flowers.

A view of Wellington Street during the First World War. An enormous queue has formed at the Home and Colonial Store, probably to buy some of the fresh consignment of cheese that is advertised as just having been delivered. The street was laid out in around 1825, with a high proportion of elegant houses, premises for a few small hat companies, and several shops. This lower part of the street remains virtually unchanged to the present day, but the shops are now in different hands.

Dunstable Lane, later Upper George Street, *c*. 1890. This late fifteenth-century building was locally called Peddar's House. John Brett farmed here in the early nineteenth century, and it was one of the last farmhouses to survive in the centre of town. It was pulled down in 1899, the site eventually being used for the building of the general post office, replacing the one in Cheapside.

Manchester Street from George Street, *c.* 1900. None of the buildings in the photograph now survives. To the left is the old Town Hall, destroyed by fire in 1919. The Franklin Temperance Commercial Hotel and Restaurant were, in 1909, offering bed and breakfast to commercial gentlemen for 4s 6d. Next door to Franklin's stood the house of Dr Horace Sworder, who was Medical Superintendent of the Sick and Convalescent Home in High Town. His house was one of the last occupied private dwellings to stand in George Street.

The *Luton News* offices and printing works in Manchester Street, shortly before demolition in 1975. The newspaper has been a part of Luton life for over one hundred years, and after vacating the Manchester Street site it moved into brand new purpose-built premises in Castle Street. The paper's present editorial offices are in Alma Street, but the printing is done elsewhere under contract. The Castle Street offices now form part of the campus of the University of Luton.

The Alma Theatre on the corner of
Alma Street and Manchester Street
stood opposite the *Luton News*
building. It was built in 1929 to
serve the needs of the ever-growing
town. Unfortunately, the patronage
did not increase with the years, and
towards the end of its life the theatre
was converted into the Cresta
Ballroom for twice-weekly dances.
Around 1962 it was demolished and
replaced by shops and offices, the
block going under the name of
Cresta House.

St George's Square, 1977. After
the east side of Manchester
Street was cleared, the resulting
site was turned into a
temporary bus terminus until
the present bus station was
completed. The area was then
landscaped and re-opened as St
George's Square. It forms an
attractive haven alongside the
Central Library at the northern
end of the Arndale Centre.

Bute Street, 1950s. It was originally laid out in the early nineteenth century and developed alongside an ancient footway leading to High Town and onwards to Hitchin. With Cheapside, Guildford Street, and Silver Street, it formed the very heart of the hat-making industry. Many of the larger hat manufacturers operated in Bute Street, including Vyse's, Warren and Sons, and Messrs A. and F. Higgins. When the railway came to Luton, the top end of the street was chosen as the site for the station.

Silver Street, 1950s. This small street that runs off Bute Street, which can be seen in the background, was dedicated to the hat industry. Mr Edmund Wiseman had premises here; he invented a Rapid Concealed-Stitch Sewing Machine, which was to revolutionize the sewing of straw hats. The building on the immediate left is the rear of the Waller Street Wesleyan Chapel, built in 1863 and demolished one hundred years later. All of the buildings have long since disappeared, and the rear boundary wall of the Arndale now runs along the left of the photograph.

One of the main roads into the town is Castle Street, shown here *c.* 1910. Many of the buildings dated from the early eighteenth century when the road was lined with small cottages. In 1139 an earth-mound castle was built by Robert de Waudari, a foreign mercenary hired by King Stephen in his fight against the barons; evidence of this was discovered when the site for the new *Luton News* building was being excavated. The Dog public house had been on this spot since at least 1806, but it and most of the neighbouring buildings were demolished in 1969 to make way for the eastern by-pass.

The Children's Hospital and Lodge, *c.* 1905. The hospital was built in 1894 as a gift to Luton from Mr A.P. Welch, JP, the opening ceremony being performed by the Duchess of Bedford. It was to serve the town until its closure during the 1970s. After standing empty for some years, it suffered serious fire damage, necessitating its demolition in 1980. Private housing now occupies the site of the hospital, but the privately owned Lodge still stands.

The Bute Hospital in Dunstable Road, *c.* 1905. The Marquis of Bute gave the site to the town, and the hospital was erected in 1882, taking over from the Cottage Hospital in High Town. It adjoined the parish workhouse, built in 1836, and both institutions combined to form St Mary's Hospital. The complete site was closed in 1992, and the empty premises now face an uncertain future.

Dunstable Road, a very busy shopping area situated about one mile from George Street, 1960s. Until the 1930s all of the shops shown were private dwellings. Luton Town Football Club has its ground within one hundred yards of this spot.

Luton fire station, *c.* 1906. Built in 1902 on the corner of Church Street and St Mary's Road, this was the station from which the fire appliances left to attend the Town Hall fire in 1919. Its engines also attended a serious and harrowing blaze at Vyse's hat factory in Bute Street in 1930. During the working day, a fire broke out in one of the lower floors of the building. It spread rapidly to all floors, helped mainly by the wooden construction of the building and the accumulation of cloth fragments and dust lying beneath the floorboards. Despite the gallant efforts of the fire brigade, eight people lost their lives when they became trapped on the upper floors. The fire station remained here until moving to temporary premises on the Park Street site of the former bus station, which had been hit by enemy bombs during the Second World War. In July 1956 today's purpose-built fire station was opened in Studley Road.

High Town Road, *c.* 1910. This was one of the first areas away from the town centre to be developed for housing during the 1830s. Much of the property was soon deemed to be unfit for human habitation, but it was to be another 120 years before any serious slum clearance began.

These underground toilets in High Town Road were among the first public conveniences in Luton and were placed handily at the lower end of the road, adjacent to the railway footbridge. They have been demolished in the last ten years.

Waldeck Road, *c.* 1955. On this busy link between New Bedford Road and Dunstable Road, the narrow railway bridge always caused traffic congestion and flooding. During the 1970s the Highways Department widened the bridge, lowered the road level, and provided better drainage. The tall building behind the bridge was Mr C. Herbert White's hat factory, built in 1906 and demolished in the late 1980s to provide a site for private dwellings.

Eaton Green Road during the 1950s is almost unrecognizable as the road it has now become. It is used by thousands of people each day as a direct route from the M1 motorway to London Luton Airport. The fields in the distance are now covered by the factory buildings of Vauxhall Motors and IBC Vehicles.

Old Bedford Road, *c.* 1905. Barely one mile from the town centre, this rural scene looks very different today, although in reality little has changed. The hedgerow to the right has gone, giving an unobstructed view of Pope's Meadow, and the thinning of the trees on the left opens the vista into Wardown Park.

Dallow Farm during demolition, 1909. Built in the late sixteenth century and considerably rebuilt in around 1700, it is believed that John Bunyan secretly preached here while on his tours. It was reported that the key of the farm was found in his personal effects after his death.

Section Two

THE RETAIL TRADE

Menday's butchers at 50 Park Street, c. 1908.

Blundell's of Luton, *c.* 1966. This local family built up a thriving business, which eventually occupied most of the site between Cheapside and Smith's Lane. Shown here is the Cheapside–George Street corner, which specialized in clothing and included a friendly coffee lounge. It was demolished in 1973, but is still fondly remembered by many Lutonians.

The household wares department of the same company occupied the area between the Plough public house and Burton's Tailors at Smith Lane. A new façade was here added to the eighteenth-century Black Swan Inn building, which otherwise remained intact. It was demolished in 1978 and replaced by the present Debenham's store.

The International supermarket in Waller Street, 1967. The town's first major supermarket, it was built in 1962 to replace the Wesleyan Chapel erected in 1863. The chapel closed in 1954 and was then used for some time as a furniture repository and overflow classrooms for the Technical College. The supermarket was itself pulled down in 1973 when the Arndale was built. The International took over one of the units in the new centre but closed within a few years.

Tesco's supermarket, also in Waller Street, 1967. The second such store to open in the town, it was built in 1963 on the site of the recently demolished Grand Theatre. It was to remain standing for just ten years before following the International into the new shopping complex. Unlike its rival, it is still trading today in the same unit.

Partridges cycle, pram, and toy shop in Chapel Street, *c.* 1973. This shop is remembered fondly by generations of Lutonians for satisfying the needs of their babies and children, always with friendly service and a smile. The business closed in around 1980, and the building is now occupied by a bank.

Occupying 34 to 36 Park Street, Panter's the butchers were to trade in the street for at least twenty years. The premises stood next to the Cock Inn, whose sign can just be seen at the extreme left. By the mid-1930s the business had moved to 30 Park Street. Note the sharpening steel hanging from the waist of the gentleman in the white apron.

An earlier butcher's shop at 50 Park Street, 1908. The photograph shows the staff of Menday's Meat Market showing their 'Quality' meat for wholesale and retail sale. It is highly improbable that meat displayed like this would pass today's health inspectors.

The cooked meat shop of C.W. Jones at 46 Park Street, *c.* 1966. During the middle of the nineteenth century this house and its gardens was the home of Charles Burr, who, with his brother Frederick, ran the brewery on Park Square. When the cattle market in Bridge Street closed, it was moved to the former gardens of this house and remained here until closure in the 1950s. The house was demolished in 1973 and replaced by a freezer company store, which was in turn superseded by the Chicago Rock Café.

Park Street, *c.* 1930. The firm of Harman and Shoosmith at first specialized in home furnishings, but at the time of this photograph their main stock-in-trade was clothing and shoes, with some household goods as a lesser line. The building was demolished during the early 1970s so that the Park Street flyover bridge could be built. The bridge is now at the height of the upper storey windows.

The fondly remembered and well loved Sainsbury's shop in George Street, 1974. As with all this company's shops, the interior was always spotless and featured ceramic tiled walls and glazed meat counters. This store closed when the company moved to a new location in the Arndale Centre. The premises were taken over by a retailer of electrical goods, and the building still stands, essentially unchanged.

John Simpson's barber's shop on the corner of Cobden Street and High Town Road in the mid-1920s. John's brother, Edward, ran a similar shop on Park Square before moving his business to Southdown Road, Harpenden. This building still exists, occupied by another small company.

Brown's, c. 1915. This was a typical late-Victorian corner baker's shop and stood at the junction of New Town Street and Albert Road. With hundreds of similar premises in the area it was an early victim of the New Town redevelopment.

An early traffic accident in Luton, or, more precisely, the reconstruction of one, 1924. This photograph shows the owner of the hansom cab, Mr Brown, at the corner of George Street and Cheapside, holding his horse and demonstrating to the photographer how his cab had collided with a private car, only partly visible here. The building housing the British Shoe Company is today occupied by a photographic and photofinishing business.

The first Luton premises of Marks and Spencer Ltd and their Original Penny Bazaar, c. 1905. The address was 40 George Street. Admission was free, and the goods, openly displayed, included Lyons' Tea. The company has remained on this site to the present day, although naturally the shop is much altered and enlarged.

The main Co-operative Society store, *c.* 1950. It had been on this site for about twenty-five years, taking over the spot from Cumberland's cattle market. The store was to serve the town until its closure in 1983. It stood empty and derelict until demolition in 1990, after which the location became a car park. There are, however, plans for the site to be turned into a new entertainment complex.

This shop, standing on the corner of Manchester Street and Bridge Street, was one of five owned by local butcher W.G. Durrant, the others being in Dunstable Road, Lea Road, Biscot Road, and Marsh Road. A public house called the Prince's Head, later the Duke's Head, had stood here in the seventeenth century. The building shown was demolished in 1976 to make way for the St George's Square area.

The Central Café in Cheapside, c. 1920. The café traded here until the early 1950s and was a popular haunt with traders from the adjacent covered market. After closure, the building was occupied by Rapido, dyers and cleaners. Next door stood Sulsky's, the sports outfitters and camping equipment specialists. All of these properties were pulled down in 1973.

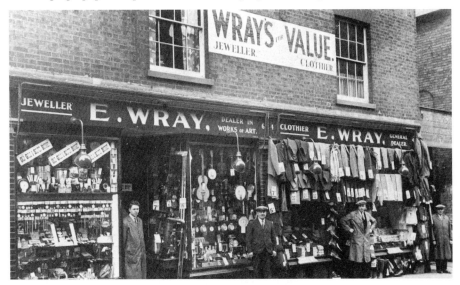

Originally occupying 4 to 6 Castle Street, Wray's had been a family business on this site since the time of the First World War. It eventually expanded, taking over the premises of No. 8. Their main stock-in-trade was gentlemen's clothing, but they diversified into selling jewellery, clocks, and musical instruments. The remaining member of the family closed the Castle Street premises in the early 1980s and for a short time ran a smaller shop in Upper George Street.

This general grocer's shop stood in Church Street close to the northern gate of the parish church and what is now the entrance to the University car park. It was demolished shortly after the Second World War.

Joseph Capp's bakers on the corner of New Town Street and Cambridge Street, *c.* 1948. Mr Capp had been supplying his customers from this shop since at least 1933 and remained here until his retirement in the 1950s.

Section Three

REDEVELOPMENT

Redevelopment in Boyle Street, 1977.

Slum clearance and redevelopment began during the 1950s in the area of High Town. This lower end of High Town had, during the 1830s and 1840s, seen some of the earliest new building in Luton. Burr Street, shown here in 1944, had been listed as containing sub-standard dwellings as early as 1850, and it is remarkable that the first demolitions of any note took place over one hundred years later.

Burr Street, 1944. There are no longer any of the original buildings left in the street, the last one being swept away before the 'swinging sixties' had arrived. One of the last buildings to go was the Britannia public house, which stood at the corner of Burr Street and Back Street.

Parallel to Burr Street and built at the same time was Duke Street. This view was photographed in around 1956 and is from Back Street looking towards Hitchin Road. The building at the extreme right with the white wall was the Welcome Stranger public house. By 1960 the only original buildings left were the Green Man public house, Saunders and Son, undertakers, and an adjoining house.

This shop on the corner of Duke Street and Taylor Street saw its last days as a bakery. During the last years of the nineteenth century, it was owned by John Wheeler, who traded in crockery. It was pulled down in 1958.

Luton's first Co-op, on the corner of Brunswick Street and High Town Road. It was opened in 1897 and has remained on this site ever since, although now with much larger premises.

A typical 1950s view of Taylor Street, taken from the corner with Brunswick Street. At the end is Duke Street, with some property already demolished, so providing a view of Burr Street in the background. Within two years all these condemned buildings had disappeared.

By 1842 Back Street was already completely developed and densely populated. Typically of High Town, it possessed no underground drainage, with the result that the water wells became contaminated by the filth seeping through the lined walls. Fever and contagious diseases were especially common, leading to many deaths every year. All this property was demolished before 1960.

Back Street during the Second World War. This view was taken close to the lower end and looking up the full length of the street. To the left of the photographer was the Co-op slaughter house; livestock was driven into the building from Back Street. The gable end of the building on the left belonged to the Britannia public house.

Midland Road and the junction with Gillam Street, 1950s, showing the grocer's shop of Mrs Rance, which before 1960 had been converted into a corner café. It was demolished, along with much of the two streets, in 1962.

Wenlock Street in 1966, a development of streets built over one hundred years earlier and close to High Town Road. These buildings were among the first in Wenlock Street to be demolished and had gone by the end of 1966.

The upper part of High Town Road towards the junction with Oxen Road. This row of twenty or so Victorian cottages is shown during demolition in 1958. They were replaced by small modern dwellings.

This redevelopment is taking place during 1977 in Boyle Street, lying between High Town Road and North Street. The cleared area was required for modern high density housing, which unfortunately has not always been the right way to develop former Victorian communities.

Latimer Road, formerly Langley Road, 1957. This area is known as New Town and mirrors the High Town area on the opposite side of the Lea valley. Both were laid out during the first half of the nineteenth century, and each suffered from poor quality workmanship and materials. The garage workshop, the roof of which is seen to the right, and one of the terraced buildings on the right-hand side are the only properties still standing today.

This view is taken from the position of the gate in the previous photograph and shows the shop of Charles Wright on the corner of New Town Street. All the properties shown were demolished in 1960 to provide space to build the new development of Kelvin Close. Just off the picture to the right is the Mother Redcap public house.

No. 38 New Town Street, photographed shortly before it was pulled down in 1956. This property was small, even by the standards of the area, having two bedrooms and one room on the ground floor. Notice, too, that there was no front entrance from the street, but there was a back door reached by the through-passage.

A general view of New Town Street on the opposite side to that shown in the previous picture. These properties are typical of early nineteenth-century urban housing and were to see their last days in 1960.

Albert Road during wholesale clearance, 1967. The public house sign seen on the left belonged to the Antelope.

The building of Kelvin Close, early 1960s. This was once one end of New Town Street, and the Phoenix public house and the Vine, which is behind the photographer, were both situated in the street. Both inns have undergone changes in recent years and are probably enjoying the most profitable period in their history.

These properties in Lea Road, photographed during 1960, were built on the site of Blackwater Lane, which had a history of waterlogging because of the nearness of the river. With inadequate foundations and unstable ground, it was only a matter of time before nature took a hand and severe structural problems developed. By the late 1940s many of the buildings were showing signs of subsidence. Demolition was the only answer, and over the next twenty years the whole area was pulled down. On the corner of St Mary's Road was one of W.G. Durrant's butcher's shops.

Lying between Lea Road and the electricity generating station were two short culs-de-sac of late nineteenth-century terraced houses, Peach Street and Alfred Street. Like Lea Road, they both suffered from ground subsidence, and the expense of underpinning and maintenance proved to be prohibitive. This is Peach Street in around 1955, shortly before the bulldozers moved in.

Alfred Street, taken at the same time as the previous photograph. The effects of unstable ground and poor foundations can clearly be seen in this picture. The majority of buildings in the street were in the same condition and were soon to be demolished.

Building of the Chapel Street flyover in 1970 meant the destruction of many town centre dwellings, particularly those in Regent Street and the south side of Stuart Street. This view is looking towards Castle Street and is taken from the top floor of the Regent Street car park.

A doctor's temporary surgery in Castle Street, 1970. The makeshift building was needed because the previous premises had been demolished for the ring road development. They were to remain here for several years until new buildings were provided after the road was completed. The photograph was taken from the site of the Dog public house, it having been pulled down in 1969.

A second view from the Regent Street car park, this time looking north, 1969. The houses in Regent Street, in the immediate foreground, have already gone, and there are very few properties left in the visible part of Stuart Street, this side of the church. King Street Congregational Church was demolished in 1970, not as a result of the future ring road, but because the steeple was found to be unsafe. The loss of this church was much mourned by Lutonians. The tower of the Town Hall is just discernible on the skyline.

Buxton Road, 1967. These were the offices of the Weights and Measures Department and they, too, fell victims to the ring road development.

Running parallel to Buxton Road was Princess Street, which was filled with houses like this. The whole of the lower half of the street no longer exists, being covered by the Magistrates Court House.

The Market Hill entrance to the covered market, *c.* 1968. The market had opened in 1925 in the redundant Plait Halls, which had entrances in Waller Street and Cheapside. This alleyway was added later, and in the market's heyday was packed with shoppers bravely dodging the loaded barrows with which the porters used to keep the stalls supplied with produce. The passage was seldom photographed, and this picture will bring a smile to the faces of those who remember it.

The last day of the old covered market, 31 December 1972. The variety of consumables offered for sale in the market since 1925 defies description, and although the new premises were to be warmer and more comfortable, the old market was greatly missed by shoppers and traders alike. Both of these pictures show stalls in the Cheapside section of the halls. For some years the market also housed a branch police station.

Church Street during the final stages of clearance, 1969. The two cooling towers of the electricity generating station were demolished the following year and the site taken over by the small industrial units of Power Court. The large hall on the left was once the home of the Luton Jazz Club, where the likes of Chris Barber, Kenny Ball and Ken Colyer often played.

At the top end of Church Street on Park Square stood these buildings, shown being demolished in 1973. At various times they housed shops trading in electrical goods, jewellery, tools and shoes. The original Curry's shop was here, as was the high-class draper's premises of Hannibal Bond. P.G. Alder, the opticians, had occupied a shop here from 1905 until 1973.

Part of a row of twelve cottages which stood in Windmill Road. At one time they had been on the very outskirts of the town, but by the time of their demolition in 1960 they were surrounded by the Vauxhall Motors factory.

The demolition of Luton's 'own' brewery during 1977. This was the Phoenix Brewery, which had first been run on this site by the Pearman Brothers from 1865. In 1869 the young J.W. Green purchased the concern and soon turned it into one of the most successful independent breweries in the country. In 1954 Green's merged with Flowers, and brewing continued until 1969, although under the banner of Whitbread from 1962. After production was transferred to a new brewery in Oakley Road, the old site remained empty until it was levelled.

Section Four

INDUSTRY

*The felt finishing room of A.R. Child and Sons
Ltd, a typical Luton hat factory.*

At the time of this photograph, in 1906, Cheapside was in the heart of the town's hat industry, with large and small factories and associated industries clustered all around the narrow streets. The railway station, with its warehouses, was close by, and the raw materials and finished hats were taken to and from it by horse-drawn carts.

A typical straw hat factory, 1906. This one was in Bridge Street and was built for Mr George Field. The adjoining buildings to the left were demolished and replaced by the motor car showroom of Dickinson and Adams, which in turn was taken over by the Co-operative Society. The hat factory itself was used by the Co-op until it closed in 1983. The whole site was cleared in 1990 and is now covered by the Bridge Street car park.

A scene inside the Plait Halls, *c.* 1888. The halls were built in 1869 to take the large overcrowded plait market away from George Street. It was the home of Luton's straw plait dealers, who bought and sold their wares sheltered from the elements. Two notable dealers are featured: Nicholl's and, in the background, Gray and Horn. The covered market took over the halls in 1925.

The inside of a typical Luton hat factory, 1950. This is the felt finishing room of A.R. Child and Sons Ltd, which was situated at 4 to 6 Williamson Street. By the 1950s, with the hat industry having already fallen into decline, Williamson Street was at the hub of the felt hat trade, with 75 per cent of the businesses connected with the industry.

This building in Windmill Road, photographed during 1963, had for many years been used as the Corporation Cleansing yard. It had originally been built in around 1904 as part of E.W. Hart's bleaching, dyeing and felt body works. The site was cleared in 1964 and is now occupied by small industrial units.

One item that the hat manufacturers required in huge quantities was clean, strong cardboard boxes for the storage and transport of the hats. There were many box makers in the town, and W. Sale and Co. of Church Street was but one of them. This building was demolished in 1957 to make way for the Luton College of Technology.

An aerial view of Lye's Dyeing and Bleaching Works in Old Bedford Road. The hat makers had originally tried to colour the plait themselves, but the use of wood and vegetable dyes gave only the colours black, brown, and blue. A turning point came in 1857 when Thomas Lye developed this site, and using the recently introduced aniline dyes, he built up a very successful business. The dyeing works closed during the 1960s and for twenty years various small businesses used the premises until they were pulled down in 1990 to be replaced by private dwellings.

George Street from the old Town Hall, *c.* 1900. Hat factories dominated the street at this time and shown here are horse-drawn carts loaded with hat boxes. All of these buildings now house shops, banks and other business premises.

The gentleman driving the 1906 model 19hp Vauxhall is possibly Percy Kidner, who was Managing Director of Vauxhall Motors for many years. The scene is in Kimpton Road outside the house that later became the company's head office. The building was demolished in the 1920s, when it was replaced by the present offices.

The heyday of Bedford Trucks was between the 1930s and 1950s, thus including the years of the Second World War, when the company was a prime manufacturer of army trucks and tanks. This is a 1930s view of the truck engine assembly line.

The sheet metal finishing shop at Vauxhall Motor, 1930s. The burnished and polished panels would be taken from here to the paint shop or assembly line.

Vauxhall Motors opened their massive canteen in around 1936, and were very proud of it. In the days before the vending machine, it would be crowded for up to three sittings each lunchtime. Out of working hours the canteen was used for recreation and concerts, the Vauxhall male voice choir giving regular performances. In 1992 the canteen was demolished, and a new recreation clubhouse opened on the Brache Estate in 1995.

The engineering drawing office of Vauxhall Motors in 1931 was a far cry from today's computer-driven design offices. The skylights provided good natural lighting, essential for manual drawing. In 1964 a brand new specialized design centre was built in Osborne Road to house all the car and truck drawing offices under one roof. Two of the designers in the photograph were to play an important role in the new building: Dick Shortland, left front, was to become chief draughtsman for the body office, while his counterpart in chassis design was Vic Cherry, right front.

The electricity generating station was built in the early years of the twentieth century on the site of the old vicarage in Holly Walk, now St Mary's Road. It was opened by J.J. Thomson (later Lord Kelvin), who was the leading physicist of the day. He astonished the dignitaries present by confessing that he did not know what electricity was! In 1948 the generating of electricity was taken out of the hands of the council and passed to the British Electricity Authority. The site was cleared in 1970.

A view of the gasholders from Crawley Road, *c.* 1954. The gasworks were opened in 1830 and were to remain here until the early 1970s, when the plant was closed and the site occupied by the West Side Shopping Centre. The centre was never a financial success and was eventually demolished in around 1991, to be replaced by a Sainsbury's superstore.

An earlier picture of the gasworks, *c.* 1920. It shows the horse transport and piles of coal ready for taking into the plant.

The control tower at Luton Airport, 1959. The airport was opened in 1939 on the site of the former Eaton Green Farm, and the airfield was used during the Second World War by B Flight of 264 Squadron, RAF, flying Boulton-Paul Defiants. In 1960 a concrete runway was built to replace the grass strip, and two years later full customs facilities were obtained. The airport commandant was based in the farmhouse seen behind the tower. The tower was built in 1950 and saw service until 1995, when a new high-technology unit, the tallest in the country, was opened.

The first factory of Commercial Cars, later Commer Cars, in Biscot Road. The company came to the town in 1906 and opened a small factory, which was over the years to expand into a thriving large employer in the town. It closed during the 1980s, and the site is now covered by private dwellings.

An early Edwardian view of Oxford Road, showing delivery vehicles lined up outside the Burgess Mineral Water Factory. The company is still trading from this site, although many of the neighbouring houses have been demolished.

A row of houses in Leagrave Road under demolition, 1930s. This was to allow the Skefco Ball Bearing Company, seen at the left, to expand; the firm has been trading in Luton since early this century. A new factory was built in the early 1960s at Sundon Park to the north of the town, and for some time both factory sites were worked. The one seen here eventually closed, and the buildings now house a host of small businesses.

Vauxhall Motors machine shop, 1935.

Section Five

LUTON AT WAR

The results of an air raid in Midland Street,

September 1942. Five people were killed and

eighteen injured.

Photographed in 1910 at the corner of Lea Road and Park Street, the Third Volunteer Battalion of the Bedfordshire Regiment are parading in Vicarage Street before marching off to their annual Whitsun Camp. The battalion's headquarters are shown on the right of the picture; it was pulled down as recently as 1975. The large building in the centre is the Salvation Army Temple, built in 1887 and still going strong today.

During the First World War, an army camp was built near Biscot Road that was to play host to thousands of troops preparing for overseas duty. The group featured here are Royal Artillery gunners. The camp had all the usual facilities, such as a YMCA hut, billiard room, canteen, and a general social hut for concerts and dances. Many of the soldiers would take the short walk on a Sunday to Wardown Park to promenade and listen to the music played on the bandstand.

Peoples Park, 1915. A detachment of army mounts are being exercised, groomed and fed in full view of interested spectators. It has not been possible to identify the unit from this photograph, but this was a familiar sight in Luton's parks during the war. An enterprising young boy with a towel-covered basket looks as though he is hoping to supply the soldiers with goodies.

A General Service wagon passing the Railway Inn at the bottom of High Town during the First World War. It is likely that it had recently arrived by train and was on its way to Biscot Camp.

The aftermath of an air raid on Park Street on Sunday, 22 September 1940. A parachute mine had landed within feet of the bus depot, damaging or destroying forty-six buses and rendering homeless about a hundred people. The houses shown were across the road from the bus station, and were so badly damaged that they had to be pulled down. A block of flats now occupies the site.

Saturday, 5 September 1942 in Midland Road. A lone raider had dropped bombs on the town, aiming for the railway station and line. It missed by yards, but unfortunately scored a direct hit on houses in Midland Road, killing five and injuring eighteen. This photograph was taken within an hour of the raid.

The first daylight raid on Luton was on 30 August 1940, and the targets were the factories of Vauxhall Motors and Percival Aircraft. The bombers continued to drop their loads as they flew away from the target, and many other parts of the town suffered damage. The bus depot received a direct hit from a 1,000 kg bomb, resulting in one person being killed and many vehicles destroyed. This double-decker bus was left suspended from the roof girders.

Local shopkeepers soon took precautions to avoid further air raid damage after three bombs fell in Seymore Road in 1940, killing two people and destroying two houses. Wooden window shutters and blast-prevention door shields became common sights. This shop in Seymore Road had already fitted the blinds by 1943.

Other air raid precautions taken included open static water tanks situated around the town, so that fires caused by air raids could be tackled quickly with a ready supply of water. This photograph, taken in 1943, shows one in Gaitskill Terrace, a poorer part of High Town. The net covering was to try to prevent inquisitive children from climbing in. The road on the right is Brunswick Street, with the Church Army Mission, which existed from 1884 to 1963, on the corner. At the far end is the lower part of Duke Street.

A blast-protection door has been constructed at this shop on the corner of Dunstable Road and Beverly Road.

The air raid siren has just sounded, and orderly queues are forming at the entrance to the air raid shelters in the town centre. These shelters formed a series of tunnels beneath Gordon Street, Upper George Street, and several other streets. These people are entering at two of the Alma Street entrances. The tunnels are still in existence and bear the original instruction notices and posters on the walls. Unfortunately, they are waterlogged for much of the time and no longer open to the public.

An example of a brick-built blast shelter at the top end of Burr Street, c. 1943. There were several of these structures in the area, and they were to be demolished only about eight years before the houses they served were themselves pulled down.

Some of the damage caused in Cambridge Street during the raid of 30 August 1940. Two persons were killed when the two houses that had stood in the gap were hit. This photograph was taken in around 1946, and to this day the view is exactly the same, with the temporary wall as it is here.

The same raid destroyed 79 and 108 Wilsden Avenue, then called Farley Avenue, when four bombs killed three people there. The houses were rebuilt after the war.

Six high-explosive bombs dropped in Strathmore Avenue, shown here, destroying five houses, but fortunately with no deaths. This photograph was taken two years later and shows some of the many oil burners that were placed around the town. It was intended that the black smoke given off would help screen the town from the air. It seems, however, that their main accomplishment was to send black specks on to all the clean washing and into every nook and crevice of people's homes. Consequently, they were not very popular.

The shops on the east side of Park Square that provided air raid shelters for the public. The steps down into the basement shelters are barricaded to prevent passers-by from falling into them.

The British Restaurant in New Town Street during the Second World War. It provided company and refreshment for both uniformed personnel and civilians. It was built in the grounds of Surrey Street School and after the war was used as part of the school buildings, before being demolished in around 1988.

The Council made efforts to provide entertainment during the Second World War, and this picture shows a band concert arranged in Wardown Park for the benefit of all. After the war the stage became a permanent fixture and was frequently the venue for plays and concerts. It was to remain until around 1960, when it was pulled down.

Marquee dances were staged occasionally in the park, although this one seems to have attracted very few dancers.

This first aid post was built behind the shops on the corner of Bishopscote Road and Alder Crescent. It probably saw little action in the treatment of war wounds, for the nearest air raid was in Limbury Road.

On the night of 21 October 1943 a stick of bombs fell on the Leagrave district. There were no serious injuries, but 400 houses were damaged. This photograph shows the result of one bomb dropped on the junction of Roman Road and Wickstead Avenue. Hundreds of tons of chalk were pulverized into a fine dust and deposited on the houses like a canopy of snow.

After the war was over and the restrictions on building materials were lifted, there was much work to be done repairing damaged property and building new roads for the new estates. Labour was short, for many British troops had yet to be demobilized, and the problem was overcome by using German prisoners of war to help with the laying of road foundations. This picture shows some of the prisoners working in the Hockwell Ring area. The houses in the background form part of Mayne Avenue.

WORSHIP AND EDUCATION

Pupils in the south playground of Old Bedford

Road School, c. 1965.

Church Street in 1957, showing the Pentecostal Church, which was demolished later that year. It was rebuilt directly across the road and is still standing. Above the church can be seen the Wheatsheaf public house, and showing above the church roof is the rising building of the Technical College, now the University.

A gang of workers outside the Mount Tabor Methodist Church in Castle Street, c. 1908. The cottages were pulled down so that an extension of the church could be built.

Christ Church from Dunstable Road, 1959. The church was built in 1856 and closed during 1975. Over the next ten years the building was used for a variety of purposes, including that of badminton courts. During the 1980s it was altered structurally and re-opened for use as offices.

Park Town Methodist Church in Brache Street, 1967. Together with most of the neighbouring buildings, it was demolished in 1973 during the clearance programme of this part of New Town.

Park Street Baptist Church was built alongside the existing Meeting House. During a fierce gale in 1866, part of an unfinished wall of the new chapel blew down and fell on to the old chapel, which then collapsed. The new building was repaired and served until 1976, when it was pulled down. The site remained vacant until a new Meeting House was opened in 1991.

On the junction of Albert Road and Baker Street stood Bailey Hill Wesleyan Church. Built in 1898, it was well known for its harvest festivals and floral shows. For a church, it was to have a unusually short life, being pulled down in the 1960s to make way for a block of flats.

Castle Street, photographed from the grounds of the Roman Catholic Church, *c.* 1960. The building in the centre was the Union Baptist Chapel, which was attended for much of his life by Frederick Thurston, a leading local photographer with a national reputation. It was closed during the late 1970s and stood empty for many years before being converted into luxury private apartments. The exterior remains unaltered.

Chapel Street, from the ring road flyover, 1969. The building on the right is the Queen's Hotel, demolished that year. In the centre is the Wesleyan Chapel and School building. The chapel was built in 1814, and the school twenty years later. It had been closed for three years when it was gutted by fire in 1979 and shortly afterwards pulled down.

Luton Technical School on Park Square, 1950s. It was built and opened as the Edward the Seventh School in 1908 on the site of the 'White House', the former home of the Burr brewing family. The school was later renamed Luton Modern School, becoming Luton Technical School in 1938. In 1957 it was demolished and replaced by the Luton College of Technology.

St John's College on New Bedford Road, *c.* 1895. In 1859 it was known as Villa School, and the headmaster was Henry Wright, who was to become Mayor of Luton in 1883. It is not known when the school was pulled down.

Queen's Square Primary School for boys in Queen Street during 1969, the year it was demolished. Built in 1857 and originally intended for boys, girls, and infants, the old school was directly on the line of the ring road development.

St Matthew's School in Havelock Road, *c.* 1966. It was built in 1874 and closed during the early 1980s to be replaced by a new school on the same site.

Old Bedford Road School for boys, *c. 1965*. Opened in 1883, it was to remain a boys' school until its closure in 1967, when its masters and pupils moved to South Luton High School. Duing the following year the front part of the building was demolished, and temporary Education Department offices were erected on the site. The boiler house and some of the rear classrooms were retained, but in 1990 the whole site was levelled, with private housing now occupying the space.

A view of the south playground of Old Bedford Road School, *c. 1965*. At one time it was hoped that the boiler house and chimney could be saved and included in any future development, but the needs of house building took precedence and the site was cleared.

Section Seven

SPORT AND
LEISURE

The imposing façade of the public baths in Waller

Street, opened in 1872.

A popular haunt for Edwardian Lutonians at weekends and during holidays was Wardown Park. The house, now Luton Museum and Art Gallery, and the park were owned by Mr F.C. Scargill, a noted local solicitor and businessman. The Council bought his property for £16,250 in 1905 and, after they had enlarged the boating lake and added tennis courts, bowling greens, and a bandstand, they opened it to the public. It proved to be a wise move, for the people of the town flocked to its green, tree-shaded areas. It is still very popular, especially at weekends.

This photograph shows the bandstand, which was the centre of attraction with its various bands. Unfortunately, it was dismantled during the 1960s.

Luton Museum and Art Gallery, taken around 1910. It was built between 1860 and 1879 and was originally the house of Mr Scargill. The museum opened here on 1 July 1931 and has continued to expand and vary its exhibits and displays. During the First World War the building was used as a rehabilitation hospital for wounded British officers.

The northern half of Wardown lake is shown here as it was in the 1920s. This end was deepened to provide a swimming area and an adjoining changing pavilion was built. Swimming galas were held from the very early days, but, although the changing pavilion still remains, there has been no official swimming since the early 1950s. The artillery piece on the left was a Turkish gun captured during the battle for Gallipoli. It was removed some time before the Second World War.

In 1872 the public baths were opened in Waller Street. By 1912 the need for a swimming pool became evident, so new public baths and a swimming pool were built on the same site. They were to remain until 1973, when they were demolished during the Arndale development.

Children paddling in the River Lea by the Moor. The Moor had been a vast area of open ground, but it was severely reduced when the two railway lines bisected it, after which it was slowly sold off for building land until all that was left is what remains today.

The official opening of the new swimming pool in 1913. The Mayor, Herbert Williams, resplendent in his chain of office, is flanked by other dignitaries as they watch a swimming gala and diving display. During the winter months, the pool was boarded over and, as the Winter Assembly Hall, was used for public dances, meetings, and exhibitions. In 1935 an open air swimming pool was opened in what was to become Bath Road and in 1965, on an adjoining site, a new indoor pool was built. The open air pool could accommodate almost one thousand bathers, with ample room for sitting and sunbathing. For the more energetic some gymnastic equipment was provided. During the 1970s it was found that the lining of the outdoor pool was beginning to deteriorate and, this, combined with a decrease in patronage, brought about its closure in 1989.

The Palace Theatre in Mill Street, *c*. 1914. Built in 1912, it served as a theatre until the popularity of the 'movies' saw it converted into the Gaumont Cinema. Early in the 1960s it closed and, after a refit, re-opened as the Majestic Ballroom. With the rise in popularity of the disco and falling attendances at dances, it was converted into a bingo hall before being destroyed by fire during the 1980s. The ruin was cleared and replaced by luxury flats.

Luton Town football team before the fourth round replay of the F.A. Cup on 3 February 1937 at Roker Park, Sunderland. The home side won the game 3–1, having drawn the first game at Luton 2–2. The team was: back row, left to right: T. Mackey, T. Smith, H. Dolman, J. Nelson, J. Finlayson, G. Stephenson. Front row: L. Rich, F. Sloan, W. Fellowes (captain), F. Roberts, J. Payne. That season Sunderland won the cup and Luton the Third Division championship, with Joe Payne scoring 58 league and cup goals in the season. The previous year, 1935–6, he scored ten goals in the 12–0 defeat of Bristol Rovers, a record of goals scored in one game that still stands today.

Winston Churchill strides along George Street in 1948, flanked by Superintendent A.J. Sear and the Mayor, Councillor William Edwards. He was on his way to Luton Hoo, where he was to address an open air rally, attended by 200,000 or more people, on the subject of independence for India.

One mile to the south of the town centre is the Luton Hoo estate. It was built between 1763 and 1771 by Robert Adam for the Earl of Bute. The Butes, together with the Crawley family of Stockwood, were the two main landowners in the parish of Luton. In 1844 the Marquis of Bute sold most of his Luton estate to help finance property deals in Cardiff. For most of the twentieth century the Wernher family were the owners of the estate. While the manor was still in private hands, Queen Elizabeth II and the Duke of Edinburgh were invited as guests each year on the occasion of their wedding anniversary.

Members of the Luton Cycling Club outside the Luton Hoo Lodge, 1886.

The Coronation of Queen Elizabeth II was celebrated throughout the country with, among other events, thousands of street parties. This one was held in Kingsland Road and was typical of them all. The houses seen on the left of the street were demolished in 1970 to be replaced by high-rise flats.

Luton has a history of parades, and a regular event was the Co-op Day festival. This one took place during the late 1950s, and among many decorated floats was this early Commer charabanc. It is seen driving down Market Hill past the Red Lion Hotel and the Conservative Club.

The same parade as in the previous photograph, only further along George Street. The Savoy Cinema has now been converted into a multi-screen Cannon Cinema.

Luton always celebrated St George's Day with parades featuring the many scout and guide troops throughout the town. This picture shows the 24th Someries St Anne's troop passing the old Carnegie Library in 1959. It is led by Hank Jones, and the flag is carried by Mick Wyatt. The young scout on the left wearing white shorts is Keith Litchfield.

The St George's Day parade, 1958. This is the same troop as before, only this time they are marching along Church Street. None of the buildings in view still stand today, and the houses on the right are on the site now occupied by the *Herald and Post* local newspaper office. The scout in the white shorts is Bill McTurk, and he is followed by David Litchfield. Brian Reeves carries the flag.

The parade of 1959, with lines of guides marching up Market Hill on their way to the parish church. They are passing the Plough public house. The entrance to the covered market is situated between Milletts and Foster Brothers. All the buildings on the right have been swept away to make room for the Arndale Centre.

The regulars of the Brickmakers Arms celebrate an unknown event, early 1970s. The pub had been trading on this site since at least 1834, but shortly after this photograph was taken it was closed down and re-opened as a licensed pool hall under the name of the Bronx. During the 1980s it reverted to a traditional public house under new owners, the brewers Banks and Taylor. They now run the house in conjunction with Whitbread, and it trades under the Brickmakers sign once again.

TRANSPORT

The old and the new: a horse-drawn vehicle

alongside an electric tram, c. 1910.

In common with many towns throughout the country, Luton had an electric tram service which was opened officially on 21 February 1908 by Baron Ashton of Hyde. A new tram depot was built at the southern end of Park Street, and a dedication stone was duly laid in the wall. This photograph was taken on the opening day and shows one of the first trams to leave the depot. The dedication stone can be seen to the right of the doorway.

The last tram ran on 1 March 1932, when the service made way for the new Corporation buses. This picture features a new bus and one of the single-decker trams, already decommissioned and taken off the rails.

High Town Road, featuring a variety of transport, c. 1910. In view are a horse-drawn vehicle, a petrol-driven motor car, and one of the new-fangled electric monsters. The tram routes were single-lined, but passing points were provided at intervals. This would often lead to congestion, especially in narrow roads like this.

The old tram terminus in Park Street, 1988. The building was incorporated into the Vauxhall Motors engineering complex in around 1964 and used as a sheet metal and wood shop. This photograph was taken just before the site was demolished in 1989. The dedication stone, which had remained in place since 1908, was removed to the museum, and its empty cavity can be seen to the right of the doorway.

By the late 1950s the decision had been taken to provide the country with a network of high speed motorways, and the first one of its kind was the M1. Luton was fortunate in that the route of the new motorway was through the western part of the town, but its building caused some disruption. This 1959 photograph shows the Leagrave High Street bridge under construction.

The former Great Western Railway station in Bute Street. This was the first of Luton's two stations and was opened on 3 May 1858. The Midland Railway station, which was opened in 1868, can be seen in the background. The Bute Street station was demolished in around 1966 and the site is now occupied by the Luton bus terminus.

Section Nine

THE HAMLETS

Cottages on Hitchen Road from Stopsley main green, 1900. These cottages are recognizable today.

Round Green was a small hamlet in the parish of Stopsley until they were both incorporated into the Borough during the 1930s. This view, taken in 1950, shows the centre of the village and what remains of the green, occupied by a police box and a men's underground toilet. The building partly obscured by the tree is the Jolly Topers public house.

The British Legion Club at Round Green, mid-1950s. It and the houses shown at the far right were pulled down before the end of the decade. For a time the empty, partly demolished houses were used by the Civil Defence for practising rescue and evacuation drill.

View from Stopsley main green, 1900. This photograph shows the view along Hitchin Road. Most of the cottages on the left remain to this day, although with some renovation. The building on the right was an ancient tithe house, which was demolished in around 1960 and replaced by a bowling alley, itself destroyed by fire within a few years.

The view from the green looking along Ramridge End Road, now renamed Ashcroft Road, 1900. The pond on the left was Common Pond and stood in front of a farm. Both farm and pond are now covered by Jansel House, an office and shopping complex.

Limbury Road, 1920s. This view is from the junction with Marsh Road, and has changed little today except for the volume of traffic.

An unrecognizable view of Nunnery Lane in the hamlet of Biscot, during the early years of the twentieth century. The picture is taken from what is now the entrance to the car park of the Moat House bar and restaurant and looks in the direction of Birdsfoot Lane. The barn on the right was part of the Moat Farm complex and has long since been demolished. Allotments now occupy the land on the far side of the barn, and private housing is built on the left.

Limbury Road, *c.* 1910. At this time, Limbury was a remote hamlet of Luton and, although insular, it was not neglected by the Luton Baptist Church in Park Street. They afforded great assistance to the village Baptists to help build their chapel in 1906. It was built by A. Cole, a Luton builder and contractor of High Town, and can be seen over the hedgerow of this country lane. This view is impossible to duplicate today as a result of housing on both sides of the road.

Black Swan Lane, *c.* 1910. This is the rear of Rose Cottages, which stand facing along Runfold Avenue. The barn facing the cottages was demolished during the 1930s. This view, too, would be difficult to duplicate, for the immediate foreground is now covered by the back gardens of houses in Kingsley Road.

Birdsfoot Lane, 1959, before the Runfold estate was laid out, and photographed from the junction with Riddy Lane in the direction of Trinity Road. The bridge over the River Lea is in the foreground, and Nunnery Lane is over the bridge to the left. Today, this road is very busy with traffic.

The rear of a pair of cottages that stood in Black Swan Lane, close to the entrance to Neville Passage. At one time they were the oldest surviving buildings in Limbury. They were demolished before 1930 and replaced by more modern housing. Black Swan Lane runs along the other side of the building.

Marsh Road, showing the shops that stood on the corner of Icknield Road, *c.* 1958. The complete corner has been demolished and is now the garage and showroom of a major car dealership.

Marsh Road, with the junction of Limbury Road on the left, 1912. With the exception of the houses on the right, which have been replaced by modern flats, the view is very similar today. The traffic has, of course, increased greatly at this busy crossroads.

Marsh Road, looking in the opposite direction to that in the previous photograph. Before 1910 the road followed the slope of the path on the left, and at the brow of the hill was only about 12 ft wide. In that year a decision was taken to make a cutting and widen the road. This cut off from the road the houses and chapel that stood on the slope, and makes access and parking difficult for the many property holders who own cars.

The Primitive Methodist Chapel that stood at the top of the cutting in Marsh Road. It was demolished in 1988 and replaced by private housing.

Further along Marsh Road to the north is the junction with Bramingham Road, where in 1920 stood the corn merchant's shop of Edward Hull. The site is now covered by a very busy roundabout, servicing four main roads, and the shop site is occupied by Neville's, the builders and undertakers.

On the other side of the railway embankment from the Marsh Road roundabout is Grange Avenue, c. 1910. The road is in a quiet rural setting. Apart from the increase in traffic and the loss of some of the trees, the view is almost unchanged today.

This thatched cottage had stood in Compton Avenue, Leagrave, from the seventeenth century until 1983, when, after it had been empty for several years and fallen into disrepair, a decision was taken to try to save it from total destruction. Over many months, the cottage was photographed and then taken apart piece by piece, each part being numbered and catalogued. It was then transported to the Chiltern Open Air Museum at Chalfont St Giles, Buckinghamshire, where the parts were reassembled into their original positions. The cottage is now once more complete and can be viewed together with many other fine buildings that also have been saved for posterity.

Leagrave in the early years of the twentieth century. This scene is probably Piggott's Lane, also known as Saw Pit Lane. Its remains now exist as a footpath between a betting office and a garden centre.

Leagrave High Street, when the hamlet had a truly rural feel about it. Piggott's Lane is just off to the left of the picture, with the Sugar Loaf public house on the left corner with Oakley Road. The pub has been trading since at least 1845, and from 1880 until 1909 a horse-drawn bus service ran from here to Luton to transport hat workers into the town.

Oakley Road, looking towards Leagrave High Street, c. 1898. The building on the left was the original Royal Oak public house, demolished shortly after the picture was taken. A new pub under the same name replaced the original and is still trading. Opposite the pub can be seen Leagrave School and the headmaster's house. The school opened in 1876 and closed in 1951, when it was then used as a youth club; it was demolished within the last five years.

A farmhouse on Leagrave High Street, 1957. The house stood at the end of a line of nine labourers' cottages known as Slate Row, also referred to locally as Tiddlywink Row. The cottages were pulled down that year, leaving the farmhouse standing alone. It is now a private residence.

Lower Green Farm on Leagrave High Street, just before it was demolished in 1957. During the latter half of the nineteenth century, it was owned by John Kinder. He was remembered as an efficient farmer but a harsh man who would not think twice about taking his whip to an errant employee.

On the opposite side of the road to Lower Green Farm, by the corner with Stranger's Way, stood these cottages. They were well over 150 years old when they were pulled down in 1957. The site is now occupied by a local sub-police station and two pairs of semi-detached houses.

Marsh Farm House on Leagrave Marsh, c. 1906. A farm had been on this site since at least 1673, when it was owned by Jonas Briggs, yeoman farmer. It was an important farm site, being situated on the old Icknield Way. Farming ceased around forty years ago, and the house now forms the centre of the Marsh House adventure playground.

Acknowledgements

I should like to take this opportunity to thank all those who have loaned photographs for the publication of this book, in particular the Home Counties Newspapers and Evening Post and Echo Newspapers groups, Luton Museum and Art Gallery, Luton Central Library, and the following individuals: Ken Cooper, Eric Meadows, Colin Collier and Geoffrey Pratt.

A sting in the tail, in that the author does not know the location of the building in this photograph, which shows the demolition of a substantial house somewhere in Luton in around 1970. It was possibly known as Bedford House, but there are no known records of a property of this name. Many houses of this type and style had stood throughout the town, having been the homes of professional people and successful hat manufacturers. The housebuilding projects of the last thirty years have been responsible for the demise of many of these properties, and this particular one has so far defied all efforts to trace and record any of its history. The author would be grateful for any information or suggestions that would help to determine the exact location of this building.

LEISURE
SERVICES

BRITAIN IN OLD PHOTOGRAPHS

To order any of these titles please telephone Littlehampton Book Services on 01903 721596

ALDERNEY

Alderney: A Second Selection, *B Bonnard*

BEDFORDSHIRE

Bedfordshire at Work, *N Lutt*

BERKSHIRE

Maidenhead, *M Hayles & D Hedges*
Around Maidenhead, *M Hayles & B Hedges*
Reading, *P Southerton*
Reading: A Second Selection, *P Southerton*
Sandhurst and Crowthorne, *K Dancy*
Around Slough, *J Hunter & K Hunter*
Around Thatcham, *P Allen*
Around Windsor, *B Hedges*

BUCKINGHAMSHIRE

Buckingham and District, *R Cook*
High Wycombe, *R Goodearl*
Around Stony Stratford, *A Lambert*

CHESHIRE

Cheshire Railways, *M Hitches*
Chester, *S Nichols*

CLWYD

Clwyd Railways, *M Hitches*

CLYDESDALE

Clydesdale, *Lesmahagow Parish Historical Association*

CORNWALL

Cornish Coast, *T Bowden*
Falmouth, *P Gilson*
Lower Fal, *P Gilson*
Around Padstow, *M McCarthy*
Around Penzance, *J Holmes*
Penzance and Newlyn, *J Holmes*
Around Truro, *A Lyne*
Upper Fal, *P Gilson*

CUMBERLAND

Cockermouth and District, *J Bernard Bradbury*
Keswick and the Central Lakes, *J Marsh*
Around Penrith, *F Boyd*
Around Whitehaven, *H Fancy*

DERBYSHIRE

Derby, *D Buxton*
Around Matlock, *D Barton*

DEVON

Colyton and Seaton, *T Gosling*
Dawlish and Teignmouth, *G Gosling*
Devon Aerodromes, *K Saunders*
Exeter, *P Thomas*
Exmouth and Budleigh Salterton, *T Gosling*
From Haldon to Mid-Dartmoor, *T Hall*
Honiton and the Otter Valley, *J Yallop*
Around Kingsbridge, *K Tanner*
Around Seaton and Sidmouth, *T Gosling*
Seaton, Axminster and Lyme Regis, *T Gosling*

DORSET

Around Blandford Forum, *B Cox*
Bournemouth, *M Colman*
Bridport and the Bride Valley, *J Burrell & S Humphries*
Dorchester, *T Gosling*
Around Gillingham, *P Crocker*

DURHAM

Darlington, *G Flynn*
Darlington: A Second Selection, *G Flynn*
Durham People, *M Richardson*
Houghton-le-Spring and Hetton-le-Hole, *K Richardson*
Houghton-le-Spring and Hetton-le-Hole:
  A Second Selection, *K Richardson*
Sunderland, *S Miller & B Bell*
Teesdale, *D Coggins*
Teesdale: A Second Selection, *P Raine*
Weardale, *J Crosby*
Weardale: A Second Selection, *J Crosby*

DYFED

Aberystwyth and North Ceredigion,
  Dyfed Cultural Services Dept
Haverfordwest, *Dyfed Cultural Services Dept*
Upper Tywi Valley, *Dyfed Cultural Services Dept*

ESSEX

Around Grays, *B Evans*

GLOUCESTERSHIRE

Along the Avon from Stratford to Tewkesbury, *J Jeremiah*
Cheltenham: A Second Selection, *R Whiting*
Cheltenham at War, *P Gill*
Cirencester, *J Welsford*
Around Cirencester, *E Cuss & P Griffiths*
Forest, The, *D Mullin*
Gloucester, *J Voyce*
Around Gloucester, *A Sutton*
Gloucester: From the Walwin Collection, *J Voyce*
North Cotswolds, *D Viner*
Severn Vale, *A Sutton*
Stonehouse to Painswick, *A Sutton*
Stroud and the Five Valleys, *S Gardiner & L Padin*
Stroud and the Five Valleys: A Second Selection,
  S Gardiner & L Padin
Stroud's Golden Valley, *S Gardiner & L Padin*
Stroudwater and Thames & Severn Canals,
  E Cuss & S Gardiner
Stroudwater and Thames & Severn Canals: A Second
  Selection, *E Cuss & S Gardiner*
Tewkesbury and the Vale of Gloucester, *C Hilton*
Thornbury to Berkeley, *J Hudson*
Uley, Dursley and Cam, *A Sutton*
Wotton-under-Edge to Chipping Sodbury, *A Sutton*

GWYNEDD

Anglesey, *M Hitches*
Gwynedd Railways, *M Hitches*
Around Llandudno, *M Hitches*
Vale of Conwy, *M Hitches*

HAMPSHIRE

Gosport, *J Sadden*
Portsmouth, *P Rogers & D Francis*

HEREFORDSHIRE

Herefordshire, *A Sandford*

HERTFORDSHIRE

Barnet, *I Norrie*
Hitchin, *A Fleck*
St Albans, *S Mullins*
Stevenage, *M Appleton*

ISLE OF MAN

The Tourist Trophy, *B Snelling*

ISLE OF WIGHT

Newport, *D Parr*
Around Ryde, *D Parr*

JERSEY

Jersey: A Third Selection, *R Lemprière*

KENT

Bexley, *M Scott*
Broadstairs and St Peter's, *J Whyman*
Bromley, Keston and Hayes, *M Scott*
Canterbury: A Second Selection, *D Butler*
Chatham and Gillingham, *P MacDougall*
Chatham Dockyard, *P MacDougall*
Deal, *J Broady*
Early Broadstairs and St Peter's, *B Wootton*
East Kent at War, *D Collyer*
Eltham, *J Kennett*
Folkestone: A Second Selection, *A Taylor & E Rooney*
Goudhurst to Tenterden, *A Guilmant*
Gravesend, *R Hiscock*
Around Gravesham, *R Hiscock & D Grierson*
Herne Bay, *J Hawkins*
Lympne Airport, *D Collyer*
Maidstone, *I Hales*
Margate, *R Clements*
RAF Hawkinge, *R Humphreys*
RAF Manston, *RAF Manston History Club*
RAF Manston: A Second Selection,
  RAF Manston History Club
Ramsgate and Thanet Life, *D Perkins*
Romney Marsh, *E Carpenter*
Sandwich, *C Wanostrocht*
Around Tonbridge, *C Bell*
Tunbridge Wells, *M Rowlands & I Beavis*
Tunbridge Wells: A Second Selection,
  M Rowlands & I Beavis
Around Whitstable, *C Court*
Wingham, Adisham and Littlebourne, *M Crane*

LANCASHIRE

Around Barrow-in-Furness, *J Garbutt & J Marsh*
Blackpool, *C Rothwell*
Bury, *J Hudson*
Chorley and District, *J Smith*
Fleetwood, *C Rothwell*
Heywood, *J Hudson*
Around Kirkham, *C Rothwell*
Lancashire North of the Sands, *J Garbutt & J Marsh*
Around Lancaster, *S Ashworth*
Lytham St Anne's, *C Rothwell*
North Fylde, *C Rothwell*
Radcliffe, *J Hudson*
Rossendale, *B Moore & N Dunnachie*

LEICESTERSHIRE

Around Ashby-de-la-Zouch, *K Hillier*
Charnwood Forest, *J Keil, W Humphrey & D Wix*
Leicester, *D Burton*
Leicester: A Second Selection, *D Burton*
Melton Mowbray, *T Hickman*
Around Melton Mowbray, *T Hickman*
River Soar, *D Wix, P Shacklock & I Keil*
Rutland, *T Clough*
Vale of Belvoir, *T Hickman*
Around the Welland Valley, *S Mastoris*

LINCOLNSHIRE

Grimsby, *J Tierney*
Around Grimsby, *J Tierney*
Grimsby Docks, *J Tierney*
Lincoln, *D Cuppleditch*